PRAISE FOR *GAWIMARRA*

'Through the fluid interweaving of personal and family histories, and regenerative encounters with Country and language, Jeanine Leane's *Gawimarra* builds a powerful archive of resistance to a colonial state that "devours itself / slice by slice like stale white bread". Jeanine bears witness to the trauma of Indigenous dispossession, punctures colonial hypocrisies, and blasts through the "layers of bulldust" left by archaeologists, linguists, historians and politicians – yet her "sharp-pointed footnotes" are also braided through with deep tenderness and openness about kin, culture, and the Wiradjuri landscape which sustains her.'

Sarah Holland-Batt

'I have heard it said that culture is like a river: we take from it and are nourished, yes, but the idea is that we must pour back into the river to strengthen culture for others too. Jeanine Leane has done this with her scholarship and creative work over decades, and now adds another offering into the repository of First Nations culture, for the benefit of all who live now and in the future. *Gawimarra* is a fierce and loving entry into the body of First Nations literature … full of beautiful, tender moments of vulnerability, as well as sarcasm and incandescent rage. Readers will be touched by Jeanine's losses and aching for language and other parts of culture, the waylaying of memory both personal and collective, and her paeans for beloved sister-friends both lost and living.'

Mykaela Saunders

'Jeanine Leane's voice soars in this unbound collection of poetry. She simultaneously tells it like it is and creates connection over those things that work to divide us. Evocative in its style, infuriating in its telling of colonial realities, and so, so warm and inviting, *Gawimarra* calls us into Circle with these beautiful Aunties, and we are honoured by their glorious stories. As Jeanine says, "what is woven will never unravel".'

Katherena Vermette

'The poems in *Gawimarra* dare speak the unspeakable, a subverted elegy in which the subject Country exists with urgency and vitality. Poet Jeanine Leane uses the act of gathering to both structure this collection and destabilise the status quo, the implications of which sever us from our world and tether us to that of the poems and all that they promise. *Gawimarra* is an awakening, a shaking to the core – and I am still shaking, long after I have put it down.'

Sara M Saleh

'Jeanine Leane's poetry undoes the colonial conventions of time that have been forced on Country, and lets Country speak as it is, and as its people hear and understand it. She asserts blackness, she rejects the controls of "historians" and academia, and she points out that she is a survivor and not a victim. *Gawimarra* is a declaration of resistance, but also a consolidation of cultural complexity and strength … This is highly nuanced activist poetry that speaks from the very core of Country with compassion, understanding, community and inviolable spirit.'

John Kinsella

Jeanine Leane is a Wiradjuri writer, poet and academic from south-west New South Wales. Her first volume of poetry, *Dark Secrets After Dreaming: A.D. 1887–1961*, won the Scanlon Prize for Indigenous Poetry, and her first novel, *Purple Threads*, won the David Unaipon Award. Jeanine has published widely in the area of Aboriginal literature, writing otherness and creative nonfiction. Jeanine was the recipient of the University of Canberra Aboriginal and Torres Strait Islander Poetry Prize, and she has won the Oodgeroo Noonuccal Prize for Poetry twice. In 2023 she won the David Harold Tribe Award for Poetry, Australia's richest poetry prize. She has been the recipient of a Red Room Poetry Fellowship and two Australian Research Council (ARC) Fellowships. Jeanine taught Creative Writing and Aboriginal Literature for many years at the University of Melbourne, where she is currently First Nations Writer in Residence.

gawimarra gathering

Jeanine Leane

UQP

First published 2024 by University of Queensland Press
PO Box 6042, St Lucia, Queensland 4067 Australia
Reprinted 2024, 2025

University of Queensland Press (UQP) acknowledges the Traditional Owners and their custodianship of the lands on which UQP operates. We pay our respects to their Ancestors and their descendants, who continue cultural and spiritual connections to Country. We recognise their valuable contributions to Australian and global society.

uqp.com.au
reception@uqp.com.au

Cover design by Lily Sawenko
Author photograph by Peter Comisari
Typeset in 11.5/14 pt Adobe Garamond by Post Pre-press Group, Brisbane
Printed in Australia by McPherson's Printing Group

University of Queensland Press is assisted by the Australian Government through Creative Australia, its principal arts investment and advisory body.

A catalogue record for this book is available from the National Library of Australia.

ISBN 978 0 7022 6632 4 (pbk)
ISBN 978 0 7022 6825 0 (epdf)

University of Queensland Press uses papers that are natural, renewable and recyclable products made from wood grown in well-managed forests and other controlled sources. The logging and manufacturing processes conform to the environmental regulations of the country of origin.

This gathering of poetry is only possible because of those who came before me – the nurturers and the gatherers who laid the ground for and grounded me in this work.

To my Aunties who raised me, taught me to love words, and encouraged me to go out into the world and seek things that were not available to them; and to Aunty Kerry Reed-Gilbert for her selflessness, determination and bravery.

CONTENTS

gawimarra gathering

Nation

ngulagambilanha returning

gawimarra

gathering

Blak poetry is
like maliyan – the eagle
unbounded by fences bodies of water
or concrete buildings –
it soars

The Gatherers

Gunhinarrung learnt to gather – map Country
with little feet as morning's pink horizons bring heat
and light to long-water Murrumbidgee women gather
in the early air when dew drips from frond and leaf
while mulbirrang nesting in hollow gum sing a new day
garru warbles – maliyan soars high above majestic
Baiame watches the balaagangirbang with wide-eyed
balis cooing on the sturdy hips of gunhis as they
gather under the watchful eyes of balaagans
skilled with time and wise with age – custodians of
place – keepers of the secrets of women teaching
the young minhis and mingaans the lore of the land
yiray marks time – rises high burns Country cobar-red
migays forage for guddi and nharrang – catch warramba
by Wollundry shores – net marrumin in the gudha of clear water
dig for cumbungi in the marshes – gather budyaan's eggs
among the reeds – search for buugang among miniature mountains
of moss – Gunhinarrung learns to look for small things that matter –
to take carefully – leave some always – to gather is to share
Gunhinarrung learnt to weave under shade of magalang
when yirinirin blows hot and dry across the plains
yiray's tangent moves above – turning time and tide –
Gunhinarrung watches the nimble fingers of migays
twine and loop braiding stories with reeds and grasses gathered
weaving words of wisdom with baskets and dillys – crafting coolamons
to learn that trees do not bleed when bark is taken – they give –
share – bear the scar to remember – to remind us
to always take carefully – gather only what is needed –
gather to return – return to gather

As steady hands sift through earthy archives – Gunhinarrung
learns to sow seeds gathered – to return to Country what it gave –
to gather is to release
She listens – gathers stories – reads them in the land she walks
Wagirra softly the balaagans tell her – tread softly on Country
they say – *Balumbambal always watching* – the ancient ones –
dead but not gone – their blood flows through us – gathers us
listen – the dead speak all the time
yiray's rays fade to a deep red girragan
arana's pale face peeks out from behind the hills
madhan is gathered and fires are lit
bilabang swirls milky white across the dark sky
night's black blanket swaddles the ngurang circle
beneath chunky blazing stars – carcoar croaks a lullaby
yiray rises and sets – arana waxes and wanes
turns day to night – Baiame watches
Gunhinarrung grows from wanggaay to ngamandhuray
now she learns to gather secrets – things that only
women know and keep deep in storage vessels of memory –
the seamless baskets of the mind where
what is woven will never unravel
Gunhinarrung becomes a wingadhan and teaches her
children to gather – to store history in safe hands
to share and gather again
Colonial collectors come steal and kill
Gatherers are dispersed hunted herded – collected
as artefacts – recorded as anthropology – listed
in catalogues – displayed as scientific specimens –
exhibits A to Z of the primitive – snapped up by
Klaatsch's camera for Basedow's missing links –
Gatherers are collected – amassed – classified –
arranged in order of hierarchy white to black

all our Gunhinarrungs become scattered words on
pages in someone else's collection – collectors do not
give back what they take
Everything is collected but memory that was gathered
stored and kept – Gunhinarrung cradles secrets between
walls that capture her – sees her history manhandled –
watches like a silent prisoner in someone else's story
as everything else is pillaged except for that held
in the intricately deep woven basket of her mind –
no man lays claim to this – Gunhinarrung listens for
the Balumbambal – only the white man thinks
the dead can't speak – she hears them – they
speak of what can never be stolen
Garinguns listen to the gatherings buried safe
as seeds in the Country of Gunhinarrung's memory
like the yinaagirbang before us we look for small things –
listen for silences – weave our own basket of
gatherings to keep safe for our galingabangbur – gather
and gather again – restore – regenerate – remember.

Black Child

Black child –
born deviant from norms of western culture.
Dispossessed like a refugee in a sea of white
divisiveness where cognitive capabilities
are measured on a colour scale according to
my phenotypic reality.
My Blackness –
marked already by your history.
So much so that you know all about me
before I am even born.
Black child –
thwarted by ingrained white perception.
My life not yet lived, but my existence already
theorised by my Black skin.
Black child –
born already labelled – swimming from
the womb against currents of conformity.
Black cross in white box records
my existence in the nation – statistically
tracked from birth to death
captive of the white square mentality.
My Blackness –
already confined by your colonial chains
redefined by white rhetoric.
Identity already ascribed from above
by a raceless ruling elite.

Witnesses

think of the memory of trees
shedding bark in layers of memory
back to forest floor to the
underground story of deep time
growth and age flourish and decay
rot and rejuvenation

Black Swan

For aeons, you sailed beyond their dreams
black swan – *rara avis* – mythical bird
skirting shores unimagined – sailing south
of impossible under *aurora australis* on
terra incognita. Land hidden east of unwritten
beyond boundaries of western rationalism
touching extreme borders of unknown
under the rim, round the last curve that
turns the flat world to a sphere between poles
where antipodean aquatics –
alter egos of white glide through
inland-flowing rivers where palette-coloured
parrots whistle not sing, where trees shed bark
and leaves do not fall, where wood does not float,
where Venus bends sunlight around the last
arc of the globe, where impossible is shattered,
where swans are black, red-beaked, serpent-necked,
satin-plumed realities wending the watered-veins
of Country flowing to her heart.
Then they came in droves of white-winged
boats from northern lands seeking to map the
heavens as they'd mapped the earth – taking,
naming, spoiling.
Your swansong rang over land,
over water – is wailing still
for *terra australis* invaded.

Weaving Glass

for Aunty Jenni Kemarre Martiniello

Aunty Jenni Kemarre Martiniello/ Southern Arrernte Woman/
Granddaughter, Daughter, Mother, Grandmother, Great-
Grandmother, Friend, Mentor, Teacher, Poet, Artist/
whose skin name is passed through Grandmother and
Grandmother's Grandmothers from Hookey's Waterhole on
the Oodnadatta Track/ where mulgas blossom yellow and
gold against red desert sand/ where your father is born to
speak three languages until english shackles his tongue/

Aunty Jenni Kemarre Martiniello/
whose parents met on Kaurna Country Adelaide and
brought two cultures together/ whose father is a mediator
for his people – your people/ whose mother was a singer
and a musician/ who became the meeting point of two
Grandmothers who might otherwise have never met/ who
was taught as a child to listen to the Spirit within – to let
it grow you into what you will become/ who grew up with
painting and stories/

Aunty Jenni Kemarre Martiniello/
who spoke the language of colour and texture long before
you went to school/ who hated the western classroom of
categories and confinement/ who learnt to make foreign
letters talk Blak stories/ who visited museums with her
father every Sunday/ who was incensed by dioramas that
said her culture and people were dead/ who carried these
images in her head/ who listened to the Ancestors to know
what she needed to know/

Aunty Jenni Kemarre Martiniello/
who was brought to Kambera by circumstance/ whose four
children were born on Ngunnawal Country/ whose parents
moved across desert to mountains to keep family together/
whose father knew her better than herself/ who taught her
to listen to her Spirit again/ who studied art and philosophy
in Kambera/ who listened to the Spirits of place that
reached out to own her/ who made Kambera her home/

Aunty Jenni Kemarre Martiniello/
who knows the Ancestors are looking after her/ joined a
writer's group in 1992/ carved out a space for Blak writers
in Kambera/ who got us all writing with ink back to ochre/
who celebrated the stories of a hundred Blak artists in
print/ who published *Black Lives, Rainbow Visions* to mark
our achievements/ who mentored many writers/ who
encourages us all to listen to the past to speak the future/

Aunty Jenni Kemarre Martiniello/
who believes there is nothing to be gained by working
for yourself/ knows you can only do well when you bring
everyone with you/ asks Spirits what she needs to do/ moves
seamlessly into the space of visual arts/ founded Kemarre
Women's Art Co-operative for urban-based artists/ knows
culture lives just as much on concrete as it does on red dirt/
thinks in three dimensions as past is present is future is always/

Aunty Jenni Kemarre Martiniello/
whose memory banks are deep and rich/ who holds her
stories and histories that no page can contain or restrain/
who is the keeper of family genealogies of place/ who can
name her Children, Grandchildren and Great-Grandchildren

in skin/ who continues the cultural tradition of extended families/ who knows that despite invasion, oppression, dispossession connection to Country is unbroken/

Aunty Jenni Kemarre Martiniello/
who takes sand from the desert melted into liquid to form solid-brittle glass/ bends it like reeds through her fingers/ weaves strength and fragility combined against the weft and warp of time/ melds the language of glass with traditional woven objects/ loops, coils and stretches coloured glass into dillybags, baskets and eel-traps/ blends old ways with new mediums to say: We Are Still Here/

Aunty Jenni Kemarre Martiniello/ Southern Arrernte Woman/ Granddaughter, Daughter, Mother, Grandmother, Great-Grandmother, Friend, Mentor, Teacher, Poet, Artist/ born on Kaurna Country living on Ngunnawal lands/ who grows seeds planted by Grandmother's Grandmothers into the future/ who can speak the unspoken into words to give us strength/ whose hands are a meeting place of what has been and what will come/ whose words, work and Spirit say: Always Was, Always Will Be Aboriginal Land/

Hardwood

eternity is hardwood
worn only over time
by the touch of wings
          the wash of rain
                    the breath of wind

Honey Gatherers

On my seventh birthday, Aunties woke me at dawn
to gather sugarbag honey from a grove of blossoming
yurana trees growing thick on the high summit of a
rocky hill beyond a fast-flowing creek behind our home.
A two-mile round trip we walked out into the
purple October morning towards the blue peak of the tallest
hill on the Bethungra Range.

Slung on a sturdy hip to cross the creek, the women bracing
and giggling at the briskness of spring water, placed on
solid ground on the other side I began to mount the ascent.
Women walked through the sun to the hum of stingless bees –
but the slope was too steep for my short step. Aunties
laughed, swung my hand, sang; promised me gum-blossoms,
honey-pods and sweet tea at the top.

My little legs ached as I trudged in the shadow
of their long strides, all the way to the summit.
Flopping down in the shade of the grove I watched the
women's hands plunge deep into treasure-trove trunks
of yellow-box gums to pull out gleaming brown combs of
sugarbag honey. My mouth gaping like a fledgling
as Aunties placed honeycomb on my hungry tongue. Each
golden drop worked its sweet spell through my baby teeth.

Aunties swigged tea from tin mugs in the sun, sucked
amber nectar from dripping fingers savouring the
aftertaste that lingers long. With sticky syrup dribbling
from my chin, smearing my cheeks and tufting my hair
I ran anointed by golden balm chasing butterflies all the
way down the slope without looking back. Hearing the
Aunties' steady step behind me I waited on a rock-throne
by the creek bank for them to come and
carry me across to the other side.

Native Grasses

Native grasses
have got to watch their backs
be careful where they put their heads up
nobody wants
them
on their property or in their garden

people call them pests
try to kill them off spread poison
pull them out by their roots
you get fined for having too many of
them
if you let them grow
they spread like wildfire all over the country
seeds in the wind

you'll lose control
they'll
take over the other story you're planting
under roses privets irises and wheatfields
no introduced species has a chance
against a stand of natives so
they
get exterminated crushed buried under concrete
blown up eradicated

native grasses
keep getting in the way of progress
you
need 90% of them destroyed to show
you own this place now
there are fines if you let too many of
them
live and flourish and rewards
if you can kill them all

still
we come back in small spaces
all over the place in
cracks in pavements respectable gardens
manicured lawns wheat paddocks golf courses
school playgrounds and other places
we're
not wanted us native grasses
we've got to watch our backs
we
keep trying to raise our heads.

Secrets

At age seven I begin to follow secrets.
They tell me everything that I
can't ask.
Secrets are like ghosts
I find them in forbidden places
when I am left alone to roam in
our ramshackle house that is never cleared
of old or broken things.
Nothing is thrown out, just locked away.
I find things
in boxes. In chests of drawers I shouldn't
open. In locked cupboards where I know
how to find the key. I find things
that are no longer meant
to be seen.
Letters. Clothes. Jewellery.
Clippings. Pictures.
Hidden stories –
waiting.

Searching

When I'm alone I search through boxes, wardrobes, sewing drawers and cabinets. All the places I shouldn't go. I touch all the things I shouldn't touch. Old letters, papers with thick black words.
Quadroon, Ward of State, Illegitimate, Orphanage, Carnal Knowledge, Destitute, Rape, Octoroon.
I can read better than I should at age seven. I don't tell anyone. Secrets help me know what big people can't say.

Steel Trap

My memory is a steel trap where
the release clasp is permanently jammed.
Things go in but they can never go
out again. They are lodged – permanently.
Stuck forever in an inescapable maze
of time, of place, of detail.
Collective history captured projecting
on a never-ending reel
across the screen of my mind.

Daisy Chain

My sister and I pick yellow flowers with black
centres on long stems from
my grandmother's garden. In the shade
we make daisy chains.
Gluey sap makes our fingers sticky as we
loop daisies together –
threading each one through the next
in an unbroken chain across the ground.

2020 Vision

… I was born on stolen land, my Grandmother's Mother
raped, my Grandmother too, my Aunties and my Mother,
I am a link in a bigger chain, I am not told what happened
in 1861, or 1887, or 1907, or 1924, or 1961, I don't need to be
I just live it …

… I am seven generations after Invasion, first
in my family to graduate from high school, my Father's
addicted to grog, my Mother to delusion, I made it through
my teenage years, I should have been right but
I still need something to get me through the night …

… I'm not cured, not even close, I am recovering,
I still smoke more than I should, but I gave up
drinking five years ago, one day at a time,
I still laugh, I still feel, I'm not a victim
I'm a survivor …

… there is no theory for Blak trauma
just sheer blunt force, hit, cut, tear, smash, break
if there are any pieces left you pick em up,
mend em, stick em back together again, go on,
no time to sit down afterwards and write a book …

… our good news never makes it to the radio, or
TV, or newspapers, or the classroom, or the office
or the street, or the bus, or the tram, or the train
we have victories, every day is a victory,
we are still here …

… they tell us there's a pandemic on, people are getting
sick, people are losing their jobs, their homes, their
lives, when they say *people* they mean *white people*,
we're still treated like flora and fauna –
people in name only …

… there's a war on, what else do you call it? Blak people
dying in police cells, women still not being heard,
girls still being raped, young Blakfellas 26 times more
likely to end up in jail than whitefellas,
they still take our children over and over and over …

… I was born on stolen land, my children born
on stolen land, there's a pandemic in this country,
began in 1788, no vaccine in 2020 – only resistance,
wake up every day stronger than all our traumas
again and again and again …

Mirrul and Guriin

ngayirr Wiradjuri ngurambang

sacred Country

dhaagun earth ash dust soil

plunge me deep ngandir
into your mirrul veins of
giilang story

let your ochres
draw
from
nganhal me

my Country's words

yinaagirbang words

dyiramadilinya badhu Wiradjuri

babanhirra guyang

cleanse me from colonial silence
kindle

hot cinders etch memories

into my garraba body

in guriin
charcoal

in mirrul
clay

Nginhaguliya Ngiyang – These Words

Wiradjuri interpretations provided by Aunty Elaine Lomas

These words cry out and I hear them—learn to mould
and shape them like clay.
There should have been a time for such words
for this word—'Nginha Ngiyang'
And a word for such time 'Guwayu'

How clunky these are as I first stumble over them.
Grappling like the child I should have been when I first
felt them—'Winhangadilinya', Sang them—'Babiyi',
Spoke them—'Yayi'

Now my clumsy tongue struggles over each new
syllable my Country 'Ngurambang' gives me.

Each one I want to devour like the sweetest thing
'Wiluray Bang Gula-dhayi' I ever tasted.
I want to suck every shred of the marrow
'Dundumbirra' from each solid sound.
I want to swallow it whole 'Dharramarra'
to know what it is to eat for the first time
I want to feel like the child born to these words
'Gudha Dhurrinya Nginha Ngiyang'

There is no logic to what memory holds
or what it releases …
and what will remain forever
unfinished …

NATION

Scatter Nation
Gather Country

Before I write another poem
I'll pause
and consider all the violence committed
by the paper it is written on.

The White Trinity

for Archie Moore

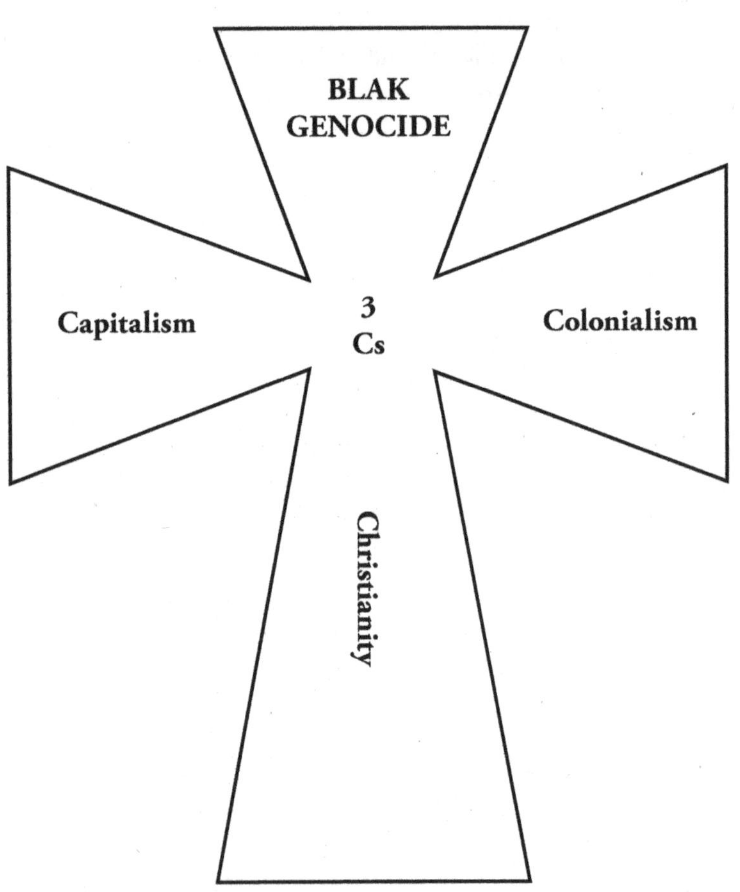

Deuteronomy Is Genocide

This is not your Promised Land.

When the lord *your god* brings you into the Countries you are invading to steal and massacre and dispossess many nations – the Dharug, Gadigal, Wiradjuri, Kamilaroi, the Kulin Nations, all Koori, Murri, Ngunga, Noongar, Yolngu, Palawa Peoples – all the hundreds of First Nations cultures older and deeper than you …

… and when *your god* has commanded you to massacre and dispossess the Countries' First Peoples you must make no treaty with the survivors or their descendants and show them no mercy.

You are living on the Stolen Lands.

Exhibition

NAIDOC week in the national capital –
a collection at the museum displays
the finest of Aboriginal culture to the settler nation.
Boxed, framed, encased, encapsulated artefacts,
wall-to-wall canvases, storyless cabinets,
soundless words captioning blank-faced photographs,
plaques written especially by historians of note
ensuring our culture is presented right –
preserved for everyone.
A smorgasbord of Aboriginal culture here –
bits and pieces taken from all around the place
labelled, cornered, polished up in chic displays
complete with commentaries from settler experts
telling our history – carving out our space.
Crowds jostle by – stare through faces, stroll
by dioramas of traditional life – mourn our passing,
quietly lament the cultural loss of us urban mobs.
Nearby a café and bar offer reprieve from the journey
through Aboriginal Australia – footsore travellers take
a break from cultural saturation over an almond
latte or a crisp flat white – hot chocolate for the kids.
In the gift store an eye-assaulting array – silk scarves,
desert prints, glossy books, tea towels, posters, jewellery,
tie pins, postcards – lots of dollars passed across the counter.
A tour group gathers – their guide assures them –
The finest display of Aboriginal culture in the nation!
All here under this roof – just for you!
Through a plate glass window, on the other side
of the lake, a different scene is framed.

Out on the lawns opposite Old Parliament House
red, black and yellow flags fly – tents ripple,
Koori kids kick a football around – a table is
set up – barbeques sizzle – cars roll in –
families pile out. A hat passed around
for the cost of the feed jingles with loose change.
Big mob gathers – banner says: **WE ARE STILL HERE!**
Embassy fire glows – Elder stands to speak – *We are still here!*
Always was! Always will be! Still here for us! Mob cheers,
breeze picks up – willy-willy twirls laughter across the lake –
dances a whirlwind of life through the still museum.

… history is not the past …
… history isn't even what happens …
… history is just one story labelled as truth …

Historians

They come out to the community in a big four-wheel drive – towin' flash campin' gear – looked like they'd be stayin' awhile – set up camp. The historians – they said they were – come out to help us tell our story.

Other fellas just left – the archaeologists – they come out to find evidence – that's what they told the ol' fellas when they asked 'bout 'em diggin' up our burial ground. Had permits they said – gives 'em permission – said it was all for the best too – discoverin' the past for the nation. After that they never said much to us – dug up a lotta stuff the first mob of white scientists found when they was here drillin' up the lake where we buried our ol' people 'round the shores.

They were the geologists – the first mob that come out – they had some papers too – said the gov'ment gave 'em permission. Told the ol' fellas they was excavatin' through deep layers of rock to find out how ol' this place really is. Might even tell us where we come from too – since they reckon we ain't been here that long. They didn't wanna talk much either – them geologists. Found our ol' people's bones like we knew they would. That's when them archaeologists come with fancy diggin' gear findin' more evidence – place is older than they thought – they dug deeper – found heaps too – us mob could tell – took a lotta boxes away. They was real shocked when they found the ol' ones' restin' place. *Discovery!* the newspapers said. We coulda told 'em but they never asked.

Then the historians come before the dust had settled from them archaeologists. They seemed a bit different at the start – the historians – other two scientist mobs stayed at the motel on the upside of town but them fellas set up camp out here next to the community. Didn't wait for the ol' fellas to come an' talk. They come over an' introduced 'emselves – said they were the historians – interested in listenin' to our story they told the ol' fellas – said they didn't wanna take our rocks an' our bones – said they wanna hear our story – our side – help us write it down – maybe make a film. Brought a feed with 'em too – the historians – started yarnin' up with some mob – makin' friends.

Said they was real interested in talkin' to the ol' fellas an' the young 'uns – somethin' 'bout the past an' future they reckoned. I'm a middle fella so they ain't interested in me. So, I just watch – not sure what to make of 'em. They had tape recorders, cameras an' a whole film crew – a lotta gift vouchers – CDs for the young 'uns, promises for the ol' fellas. Been waitin' long time to tell our story – the ol' fellas – white scientists come an' go – ol' fellas still waitin'. Thought the historians might be gunna do it – seemed real genuine like they wanna know – talked real nice to mob – the historians.

But not me – jus' the ol' fellas an' the young fellas. So, I sit back an' watch 'em work – them historians – they sure wanna talk – ask a lotta questions too. Trouble is they wanna start the story halfway through – use a lotta fancy words like *periodisation* – confusin' the ol' fellas. Could see they weren't listenin' – writin' a lotta stuff down though. Other whitefellas used to dig up our past with shovels an' drills – we could see what they was doin' an' what they was takin'. Couldn't see what the historians was doin' with our words.

I watched this one – seemed to be the leader bossin' everyone about – always talkin' in front of the camera. Well-dressed blonde she was talkin' up real nice to some mob they picked out for their film. I watched her filmin' them fellas – starin' through two hundred years with blank blue eyes while her tape recorder was feelin' nothin' – writin' down every word they say – recordin' their lives – their secrets. Can't hear so I jus' watch her fill up them blank pages.

They left after they finished recordin' an' filmin' in a big cloud of dust jus' like they come – wavin' goodbye an' promisin' to come back with the book an' the film an' some big changes. *Soon,* they said – the historians – *these things take time but we'll be back – promise* – they said.

Ol' fellas an' young fellas waitin' – hopin' – been a long time now. Back in the community – some of the mob wonderin' if they shoulda talked to them whitefellas – told 'em so much. Started arguin' 'bout it after the historians left – fights got worse while they was waitin' for 'em to come back. Some of the ol' ones passed away an' the young 'uns still got nothin' to do except wait – still waitin'.

Then I seen 'em one day – the historians – not back in community – on the TV they were – recognised 'em straightaway up there on the big screen – that blonde one struttin' across the stage receivin' an award for a book. *Groundbreaking discoveries in Aboriginal history,* they say as they hand her a cheque. *Sixty grand* eh? Lotta money. No book or film ever turned up here – mob still waitin'.

TV says book says all Australians can learn a lot from this story – move forward as a nation. But we already knew it an' we ain't goin' nowhere. We still ain't got no jobs – no more money – ol' ones still gettin' sick – young fellas still ain't finishin' up school. I look out the window an' see my mob still waitin' but I know they ain't comin' back – the historians – our story already been written now an' white Australia's busy readin' it – learnin' a lot 'bout Blackfellas an' our rich history. Sure is rich all right!

Back here mob learnin' too – learnin' historians got short memories – learnin' how Blackfella history works 'round this Country – works real good for historians.

Sista-Cuz: Tracey Phillips 1961

Sista-girl – Tracey Anne Phillips – Ngunnawal/Yuin woman
Daughter of Uncle Tom and Aunty Sally
Sista to Pearl, Stephen, Billy, Michelle, Marty, Danny and Sandra
Mother to Ronnie, Bec, Danny and Michael
Grandmother to their children
Aunty to many, Sista-girl, Cuz and Friend who lives on
Country in Kambera.

Born in the spring of 1961 – in the Year of the Ox like
me – your Wiradjuri Sista. We share the same river – the Murrumbidya
that carries the stories of our Mothers and Grandmothers.
We share the same suburb in Kambera where concrete, asphalt and
invading english gardens are no match for what speaks to us
from below.

They sent a white man into space in 1961 Sis, and on earth
their white sisters, wives and girlfriends were hailing the
contraceptive pill as a revolution. On Ngunnawal and Wiradjuri
Country – like all the other Blak Countries under the stolen
nation – our Blak Mothers were trying to keep their children –
like you and me Sis.

During the feminist revolution that splattered across
our black and white TVs all through our childhood Sis –
white women trying to get out of the kitchen and burn
their bras. Our Mothers lived in tents and tin-sheds and
cooked for us on open fires without complaining about the
heat. Couldn't afford underwear to burn so they could feed us.

That's you and me Sis in the classroom under the cross
in catholic school tunics, scrubbed up shiny and clean,
hair in tight braids – two little five-year-old girls, listenin'
to the Irish nuns tell us our Country is young and we're
not here anymore in 1967 while they're all singin' on TV
– *Aborigines want to be Australian too!*

We bit our tongues then didn't we Sis, coz it was better
than getting beaten. We watched our old ones die tryin'
to make the world a safer place for us. This year we'll both
turn sixty Sista-cuz and our tongues are free now. We
wear the lines on our faces with pride like a
map that our children will follow.

On International Women's Day

This year like every other the white women will
come out to celebrate Women's Day.
There'll be purple ribbons, T-shirts, banners, flags
slogans saying *Women of the World Unite* –
there'll be corporate breakfasts, achievement awards,
champagne and motivational speakers.

You're just like us
the white women at my work tell me when I
decline their invitation to celebrate. *Just like us …*
only … well … we're all the same under the skin.
They tell me not ask me.
Between my skin and my womanhood
and my womanhood and my skin are blood and bone.
My skin is Blak. Inside is my womanhood.
Do I peel my skin from my body
or wrench my body from my skin?
Either way feminism will make me bleed.

I was destined Blak and conceived woman.
I am neither Blak only nor woman alone.
I have too many Sistas without happy endings
too many Aunties who've hit the wall
seen too many Mothers weep for lost children
know too many women who will only wear purple
in bruises on their faces and bodies
to celebrate this day.

While We're Waiting for Armageddon

We've been promised several endings while we're
waiting for judgement day since the prophecy of Armageddon –
the ultimate struggle between good and evil.
Dante predicts a raging inferno,
Yeats sees desert birds, darkness descending, a grotesque beast
slouching to Bethlehem to give birth to a monster not a saviour.
TS Eliot says not with a bang but a whimper,
Robert Frost thinks of fire and ice,
Edwin Brock said the twentieth century would kill us but
that has been and gone.
Nostradamus predicted a 'King of Terror' in 1999, but he is late
all other doomsday dates have been a no show.
Michelangelo had us descending damned into hell.
Edvard Munch saw a silent scream before a purple sky.
Ronald Reagan told us in 1980 that we may be the generation
that sees Armageddon –

Artists, poets, prophets and politicians promised us
the end of the world.
While we wait climates change, continents heat,
ice melts, birds drop from the sky, more animals appear on extinction
lists than living on lands, rivers are fished, oceans polluted,
wars are fought in the name of peace. Things fall apart.
Bit by bit the world is destroyed by small acts of forgetting.
The centre does not fall in a blazing comet of glory to earth
to be filmed as fodder for social media. The centre crumbles around us.
Each tiny hole goes unnoticed.
The world will die by denial – end in oblivion – annihilated by amnesia
while we're waiting to see it on the news the next day.

2020: Viral Reality

the shell cracked open the world shuddered like an oyster
exposed to an enemy that armies cannot kill
a real virus goes viral not just on the internet
borders that we couldn't see before
shut like iron curtains leaving loved ones stranded across state lines
cities halt to a standstill
our wide brown land contracts to the size
of your little piece of Australia if you own one
and if you don't Country around you shrinks
to the size of four walls
governments spawn anxiety urging people not to panic
we're all in this together – just don't
go to check on your neighbour
be in solidarity, unity and isolation all at the same time
some lives are worth more than others
toilet paper is worth fighting for
hands clasped in the sanctity of sanitiser
supermarket shelves stripped bare
schools close – kids stay home staring at screens
we wear our masks on the outside now –
a muzzled world of half faces
blurred days – tomorrow and tomorrow and tomorrow
the world limps in this pace from day to day
lives on hold jobs insecure
the new reality is virtual as we zoom in and out of each other's lives
– no more holding hands hugs spread germs kisses can kill
we stare at a shrinking horizon into an uncertain future …

Eyes of the Other

Parliament is sitting late this evening. Debate
has raged. Politicians sit down to a meal – been
a long day of carefully crafted words – semantics are
crucial. Dominating today's agenda is
live exports – everyone is careful not to say sheep,
and Manus Island – the inmates, detainees,
immigrants, asylum seekers, refugees.

Tonight, on the menu it's veal. A few days ago
it was a new-born bobby calf, but veal sounds
better than stolen baby, waste products of dairy
sound like something in need of disposal and
processed is cleaner than slaughtered – blood is
a long way from this table. Meat is tender, barely
pink, almost white, less than a week between womb and
plate, no sunlight in between.

Veal scaloppini sounds painless, easy on the
conscience. It looks pretty in its dish,
arranged silently a long way from the scream
at the end of the conveyor belt after a long night
in a cold pen. Atop the meat is cream – dairy fresh
from a cow just birthed a healthy bull-calf. She
lumbers to a bale, eyes searching, udder bursting,
teats weeping undrunk milk, is hooked to a
machine – good for another five to seven years milking
and just as many calves before the pet food factory.

Stolen pastures grow succulent sheep and this
week's meat-pack is no exception. Tonight, at home
it's barbequed lamb chops for the ordinary
Aussie's dinner – six o'clock news as the backdrop.
Manus Island again! Or is it Christmas?
No matter – it's all the same thing!
Cameras roll in on brown people storming a fence.
Table talk turns to TV. *Don't they behave badly?*
Bit like animals really? Government should do
somethin'!

Sweeping scenes tell nothing of long, slow
days, cold crowded nights, hungry children,
substandard sanitary conditions, war-torn
homelands, loved ones missing. Fuzzy,
hazy lenses flicker past a surly unkempt mob
in prison garb, faces obscured, gazes unmet –
pain unfelt. *Same old same old* – someone grumbles.
Yeah! No more boats! says another. Glasses clink –
plates are refilled.

TV pans to commercial – box lights up with a
festive crowd feasting on Aussie lamb.
That's better! someone says. A majestic chorus
sings out in piercing falsetto of beaches, budgies
and lamb barbeques. A woman twirling a platter
of chops assures viewers that this sweet flesh can
bring *all* Australians together – decades of
discord can dissipate with the white smoke
rising from the lamb on the barbie.

Back to the news – Indigenous communities –
again! Eyes go to plates. Faceless figures,
disgruntled youths too far away to see faces
on the screen. *We said sorry!* someone said.
Yeah – people need to do something for themselves –
don't they? says another.
Leave it to the pollies that's their job – right?
We pay taxes and they get paid heaps!

And they do. Sitting late all week, there are tax
cuts for big business to discuss, the royal commission
into banking, United States foreign policy, offshore
investments … live exports – again, Indigenous
communities – as always!
Tonight, on the menu it's pork belly –
meat is tender and beige – sliced clean off the bone.
Resembles nothing of its original form
served under sauce. Eyes long discarded.

They Said I Could Be a Feminist

In the '80s they said I could be a feminist
if I didn't talk
about Blackness because that fragments
the movement and they said I could join
in if I believed in the oppression of all women
they said solidarity would protect me but I
still got asked why I walked out at night
in *that* part of town which is where I live.

They didn't want to hear
the history of rape
the history of rejection of who I am
the history of terrorised incarceration of
myself or that I am
the history of battery and assault and invading
armies against whatever I want to do with my mind
and my body and my soul and
whether it's about walking out at night
alone
if I need to be
by myself
thinking about life or thinking
about children or thinking about the world
disclosed by the stars and the silence
I know I could not walk out.

I am the wrong skin
the wrong sex the wrong age
the wrong nose the wrong hair

the wrong need the wrong dream
the wrong demographic in the wrong place.
I am the problem everyone seeks to solve.

Twenty years later
a middle-class white counsellor says,
Stuff happens! I'm here to help you deal with it!
I say, *Yeah stuff happens! Like magic …*
and shit, like assault, like rape …
like racism! All in unequal proportions
She says, *Why are you so angry?*

They said I could be a feminist
that they'd meet me at the intersection but
the centre keeps moving.
Do I bleed the woman from my Blackness?
Or drain the Blackness from my womanliness?
What do I sell at this crossroads –
my soul my skin my sex?
Unbroken white lines stretch beyond me.

O Australia

O Australia I want to follow the transit of Venus/ sail around the corner of the world/ discover your *terra incognita*/ catch the first fleet/ get a ticket of leave/ take up land/ cross your great divide/ unlock your pastures/ dive into your jewelled sea/ Australia I want to chart an inland river that leads to your opal heart/ be a part of your Australian legend/ work in a working man's paradise/ have a fair go/ ride to wealth on a sheep's back/ spread myself out across your wide sandy beaches/ be a bronzed Ozzie/ feel you move from beautiful one day to perfect the next/ sing suburban sonnets to summer sprinklers/ be swaddled in the southern cross of Eureka/ tattoo freedom on my forearm/ weep for your droughts and flooding rains/ Australia I want to sing I come from a land of plenty/ be a happy little vegemite/ Australia I want to find my piece of you/ sing I am one but many/ advance you fair/ say you'll be right mate/ feel your blue sky lap my ankles/ see you shimmering through my windscreen/ say you are the wide brown land for me/

O Australia I want to drive through your layers of bulldust/ untwist your furphy-history/ pull the wool off your eyes/ tell you you're dreamin/ hang your dirty laundry on a rotary clothesline/ get the Black velvet out of your closet/ dig deep down under where the bodies are buried/ stitch up your open-cut mines/ Australia you are sick at heart my Country/ Australia we watch our people die/ Australia you are a poor fellow my Country/ what you hid is surfacing/ what you beat is defending itself/ what you scorched is burning you/ Australia there are Countries screaming under your nation/ what you killed is haunting you/ what you silenced is talking up at you/ Australia listen to your ghosts/ hear that terror still nulling you/ Australia what you buried is rising/ Australia you killed your first-born/ Australia you are not young and free/ Australia we want to cure your national amnesia/ Australia we want to wake you up/ ease your cored-out heart/ Australia we want to sing you/ Australia we want to let you Dream again/ Australia you keep drowning out our voices/ Australia you won't know us/ see us/ hear us/ listen.

Read the Rivers

Ice melts. Fires burn.
Australia is a furnace. Code red alert
painted across the horizon.
It was summer all winter. Snakes came
out in July. Body rhythms confused.

Will our children still exist by the time
this is irreversible? Will they live in a time
when the only ice in the world is pulled
from the guts of a machine?

Will grandparents be the ones to break
the myth that the earth was not always
burning? Or that the sea was not always rising?
That once there were trees, birds, fish and animals
That once there were islands
swallowed by the sea.

Rivers are living bodies that have no human rights,
rivers are archives of Country,
rivers are veins that go to the heart of land.
Hold these imprints in your memory,
don't let them fall from your view.
Floodplains are now harvested, our rivers
are troughs for capitalist pigs.

Decline is not the natural order of things,
we know the earth is warming,
fresh water is shrinking, saltwater rising.

We know fish are dying, animals disappearing,
birds falling from the sky.
Please pause to think …
Extinction is now.

Heal Country. Heal ~~our~~ Nation.

The nation is a masculine myth that makes all our Countries sick. There are many examples of this. The Kalari – the living water in the central west on Wiradjuri Country was renamed the Lachlan River. To the north of the freshwater cradle of Wiradjuri Country the Wambool was renamed the Macquarie. The modern nation is full of this name-calling. Most cities – Sydney, Melbourne, Brisbane, Adelaide, Darwin, Perth all bear the names of dead white foreign aristocrats; the highways and byways that dissect, desecrate and mutilate living Countries bear names such as Hume, Macquarie, Mitchell, Newell, Brockman, Stuart, Sturt – all white men with dubious reputations.

When you take away someone's name you don't just take away a word. You take away spirit – heart and soul. When you change language from one that names all things as living to one that makes all things, things only, it causes diseases, chronic illnesses, ongoing injuries and sometimes even kills the things that were once living through their names.

That's what happened here when the invaders came permanently to our shores in 1788. They stole lots of things – our lands, our waters, our languages, our children, our dignity, our freedom, our birthrights to live on the Countries our Creator Spirits made for us.

They also stole names from Country. Sometimes they named over things. Sometimes they took names from one place – that was their place – and put them somewhere else where they don't belong. Like when they took a name from the Country I belong to – Wiradjuri Country on the Murrumbidgee River near Gundagai called Willie Ploma – a place of big possums and moved the name to a farm where they ran sheep and cut down the trees of the possums. Mostly they just changed names to their own language, like Australia – the name that erases all our Countries.

Our Countries – Wiradjuri Country where I was born; Ngunnawal/Ngambri where I lived and worked, raised my children for thirty years; Wurundjeri Country where I now live and work – are all living bodies. They have blood, arteries, veins, pulses, bones, limbs – arms, legs, elbows, knees, shoulders, feet, hands, fingers, toes that flex, bend and move as one like a body. And organs – like hearts, bellies, hips, wombs, breasts. Countries have souls and minds.

When you change something from a living subject of conversation constantly in dialogue with their surrounds – the animate landscape and their children, the people living on Country – and make it an object of information you are starving it slowly of cultural nourishment. You incarcerate and isolate it from its family and relations and of the life it once had. You make it sick, in spirit and in self.

In 1820, colonial governor Lachlan Macquarie renamed a vast body of water spanning Ngunnawal/Ngambri Country to the border of Wiradjuri Country called Weereewa – meaning hard water or salty water – after a sick, philandering, laudanum-addicted British monarch called George IV. In renaming Weereewa as Lake George, Macquarie forced masculine gender and contamination on a living body of water.

Once brimming with water that lapped against the side of what is now the highway, Weereewa is now completely dry, and has according to the short history of place written by invader-settlers 'misbehaved' ever since. It has claimed the lives of several settlers who trespassed on the waters it once had leaving many people wondering why. It is reported by white scientists to have vicious waters that turn in on people unpredictably. Now it is seen mainly through settler eyes as a useless dry bed.

But it is not 'misbehaving'. It is remembering. It is grieving. They cannot understand that its waters may have seeped from one world – the one they have invaded – to another. They cannot understand this because they can only live in one world. They can only exist on one plane.

The psychogeography of our Countries remember who they were. Before nation.

Australia is sick with loss of self. This nation is not ours and was and always will be a myth to us until the toxic naming practices are erased from its body.

Our Countries cannot heal until their names are given back.

Fortress Australia

Last night I watched the sun eclipse the
moon in the night sky/between them earth
no longer as we know it/lovechild of star-
crossed planets/Australia devours itself/slice
by slice like stale white bread/a cannibal of
states and territories/nobody's celebration
of a nation/a loose-weave federation says
fuck-this-union/jack this mate ship has
sailed/no more boats/colonies are revolting

White identity politics implodes in vira
pandemic/soft borders harden/Queensl
hospitals are for Queenslanders only/N
has gold-standard contact tracing doesn
need to shut down/WA says who needs
the eastern seaboard/SA boasts they're
virus free/Tasmania's an island nation/
Victoria under a second
wave severed like a
leper's limb/no time for
Samaritanism/not all
stars shine equal in the
southern cross

A woman is raped in parliament
house/under a hills-hoist flag/law
men of the highest order/can't
remember who irons their shirts/
between private-school-privilege and
bowls of prawns/the world is not
everyone's oyster/the milkshake of
consent is thrown back in another's
face/it takes wealthy white women
to get assaulted before people listen/
PM's wife says think about his
daughters/could be them

How good is Australia/PM sleeps smugly under
a doona of delusion/his wife doesn't ask him to
think brown children could be his daughters/
he can decide who comes here/this is a fortress/a
hairdresser on the Gold Coast gives health
advice on anti-vaccination/the elderly are
malnourished/more politicians and athletes are
immunised than the vulnerable/what dystopia
are we talking about now

Blak Lives still don't Matter/supporters
are labelled statue-busting anarchists/
women are still not being heard/social
justice activists are radical Marxists/
wokeness and political correctness cause
white genocide anxiety/it's everyone for
themselves/citizens are locked in/asylum
seekers locked out/loneliness breeds
totalitarianism/last night I watched the
moon eclipse the sun in the night sky/
between them fortress Australia

I keep Wiradjuri Country deep in my heart
as Australia the nation invades my body
weighs heavy on my back
tries to infiltrate my head

ngulagambilanha

returning

Hostages

The kidnapped memories of
Aboriginal people are hostages
beneath this white settler mythscape.
Hear us now. Release our words.
Set us free.

Biladurang Untranslated

You stop me in my tracks when I
see you in the Grand Gallery of Evolution
at the Muséum national d'histoire naturelle
on Rue Geoffroy-Saint-Hilaire – a mythical
place so the citation says where modernity meets history
and science tells the story of great adventure.

I trace you
from top to toe and back again
with my eyes among 7000 species collected
and displayed. *Ornithorhynchus anatinus* –
phylum: Chordata; class: Mammalia; order:
Monotremata. Australian platypus.

On a river a million miles away
where I walked as a child you are biladurang.
My Gunhinarrung stooped with stick,
black hair turned to ash, still walking the river
told me your name. From Mundarlo Bridge
to the Nangus floodplain we'd watch you arch
and dive your rippled story deep into the dark water.

Derrida said,
Every text remains in mourning until it is translated.
I wander through these display cabinets of
butterflies and moths pinned to boards, reptiles
marinating in jars of ethanol, birds and animals
stuffed, splayed out and labelled in Latin
behind glass and wonder.

Are you not already known biladurang,
on Country that birthed you – shaped you
through lands and waters. Named you through story.
On the other side of this translation
a river somewhere will remember you –
or a mountain, a ridge, a plain, a gully or a creek
will know you by your name.

Biladurang it's your capture you mourn behind
those glass eyes that stare out at me.
When I speak your name out loud – biladurang
I give it back to you from the river where I
first heard it – the river that still remembers you
free and untranslated.

Unfinished Business

I came back decades later to rooms she'd cleaned
in ruins of a homestead on the river of
my Country. Cast-iron gates built on years of
bumper crops, golden fleeces, free labour, swing
open on rusty hinges like pages in an unfinished story.

Native grasses reclaim the poplar-lined path to
the manor. Bluebells grow across unmarked graves
in the garden of the mansion of many rooms that
sucked youth from Blak women till there
were no more many hands to make light work
and it all fell apart.

I was a child when Aunty sat me on her lap
and told me of this life I didn't have to have.
Days rising before the sun, endless baskets
of washing, ironing, mending, tending babies
born to rule. Of bent backs, fingers worn to
the bone, floors scrubbed, linen starched, shirts
pressed, broom straws and dignity worn to the nub.

She never told of hungry nights in cold rooms
listening for every creak of the floor, every
shadow passing the door that might enter rooms of
sleeping servants. Years later I read about that in
someone else's archive and raged at what
happened between these walls when I could
afford feminism, Marxism, humanism and every
other ism built on broken backs of the last generation.

Lacking her generous spirit that forgave the past
I came back to scream at the walls, shout back at the
silence. I walk towards boarded windows, locked doors
an old straw broom worn to its core, fifty years
out of her hand never did clean the blood from the
land or the stains from their hands. I come back now to
this ground of unfinished business, leave the gates open
when I leave – swinging on rusty hinges.

Ngurambang Yali – Country Speaks

Wiradjuri interpretations provided by Aunty Elaine Lomas

It's been too long since I sat on granite in my
Country and thought

Too many years since I breathed this air—
Bunyi-ng—ganha
Felt this dirt—Ngamanha Dhaagun
Smelt this dust—Budha—nhi Bunan

Listened for the sounds of her words that say
'Balandha—dhuraay Bumal-ayi-nya Wumbay
abuny (yaboing)'—History does not have the
first claim. Nor the last word.
Nghindhi yarra dhalanbul ngiyanhi gin gu
You can speak us now!

Unsung

for Aunty Kerry Reed-Gilbert 24 Oct 1956 – 13 Jul 2019

I think I might see you when I walk out this morning along the street we used to share. Winter is cold in Kambera. Icy winds off the mountains, sleeting rains, sun-fired fogs that hang low and late bring the birds down into the hollow where the suburbs are now.

They come in droves. Rainbow lorikeets, king parrots, crimson rosellas, galahs, gang-gangs and sulphur-crested kuracca – your totem.

It was not meant to be. I turn the corner and the wind hits me cold and sharp in the face like reality. You are not here in this house with jasmine-clad front fence, lilies by the door. A place of Aunties and grandchildren. Where us mob gathered to write. Talk our Blak lives. Celebrate the strength of us – Blak women.

Early on the morning of your passing a thick cloud of kuracca swept in flying low above your old house, calling loud. Taking your spirit home. Releasing all that was unsung of you across the open sky.

Living Literature

trees are old stories
pods and seeds are words that grow
bark chapters fall to earth
turn to dust scatter and renew
wood is a deep archive
an ancient custodian of memories

Links

Perhaps the women were right. To know at the time that I am a link in a bigger rape chain might have stopped me from getting on with *it*.

> *It* is success – freedom
> that they both craved and feared.

There's a picture of you. Looks like me. Or you as me as you. History lands on your face. On my face. Mine as yours as mine. You as me as you.

Archive of Self

When I want to remember
something beautiful
I don't take a picture
I close my eyes
snap its image in my brain
file it in my heart
use my body as a lens
to look back through
the archive of myself.

Yanhamambirra – Release

Wiradjuri interpretations provided by Aunty Elaine Lomas

The space of my emptiness is a chasm so deep so wide
I'll fall to endless nothing without your words to cross it.

I have starved for you to feed my soul nourish my
blood to strengthen my bones. ngadhi bagurany
dhalbur (ngadhi bagurany dhalbur)
I have craved for the taste of your sound on my
parched lips the drip-drop of your coolness on my
parched palette. dulba nginhu balaba ngandabirra
mugumaga (mugumaga)
Ached for you to speak to sing to sound to shout
release your syllables to the air that I can breathe you
drink you grasp you. murunwiginya ngindhu,
yirbadharra ngindhu, mulgamarra ngindhu.
My tongue thick – a heavy cringing prisoner bashed
and battered by two hundred and thirty years of
colonial submission stalls stubborn over your form.
For too long my mouth paid lip-service to english
been a slave to grammar prisoner to punctuation
handmaiden to pronunciations servant of prim
proper and poise.

Life sentence lifted my tongue can liberate my heart
with these words from you
I am Wiradjuri … Baladhu Wiradjuri
I am proud … Baladhu Dyiramadilinya
I am here … Baladhu Nginha

Wiradjuri Dictionary

My 57th birthday present from my son

ngulanyin

is a Wiradjuri dictionary

I sit before this brick-like book its

covers radiating yellow like the sun *yiray*

outside my window

between these white pages are Black words

ngiyang *yuwin*

that rolled from my Grandmother's Mother's

Gunhinarrung *Gunimbang*

lips but never graced mine

I pore over this silent object –

ache for it to speak its words to me

press my ear to smooth soundless

pages that they might breathe *bunyingganha*

these words *badhu Wiradjuri*

through me

in me *mulunma*

that I might hear their music play

over my soul

dhulubang

like a love song

ngurrbul

gudhi

Forced into Images

a poem to my colonisers

Body is water is body. Not a symbol. Or a metaphor. Body
and water are one – same body. Together.
A river is a body. A body is a river.
Rivers have arms. Elbows. Mouths. They bend. Turn.
Chortle. Sing. Rage. Nurture. Run. Lie in a bed. Give life.
Destroy it. Remember everything.
Rivers are contested spaces.
When our river bodies are cut up, dammed,
straightened out and polluted we feel it. Rivers of my
Country run inland like veins and arteries to a heart.
What happens when these are cut, broken, poisoned,
severed, savaged?
When a river floods it remembers its former self before it
was forced into an image of not-self. I am counting all that
you took in the numbers you brought. Can it be put back
together again – mended – sewn up with thread leaving
only a memory of rough seam backstitching over time.

Blak bodies are contested spaces.
Invaded before we are conceived. A battleground of images.
Our journeys in your imagination begin long before we
hit the road. Skin is everyone's business. Blak bodies are
public consumption. Food for white thought. Chewed up.
Shat out. Re-consumed. Forced into images not of our own
devising. Prisoners of the mind.

Blak bodies are for theorists – linguists, anthropologists,
historians, ethnographers, white scientists. We make data,
statistical reports, policy fodder, textbooks, portraits,

postcards, tourist brochures – the stuff of images. Noble savages, wanton women, Blak jezebels, murderous heathens, witch doctors, baby-eating cannibals. An arse-hanging-out-of-their-pants drunken fringe-dwelling bum. Australia is a violent translation. It's not my myth. It's yours. Countries invaded for a nation. A land of grids and gradients. Maps and clocks. Of mathematics and science that cannot read a body that might be made of water and sand and soil. Things that have more names than I could write on this page if I could ever know them.

I am a bad translation. Colonial abomination. A sharp-pointed footnote that jabs at the sole of the respectable body of history treading on the page above it.

Nation forces its images over our Countries. There is no word in my language for environment. Or climate. Just Country. Ngurambang.

Rednecks believe that they have conquered an empty land for progress and prosperity. Greenies want to restore a mythic environment to a pristine wilderness of unpeopled space. In between this colour-politics I am erased from the picture.

Nation tells me my glass is half full.

I say I understand your colonial fractions that cut up land, rivers and bodies. Half. Quarter. One-eighth. One-sixteenth.

If you were not here, I would not be half in the nation that silences me – divides me with numbers – cuts me with glass. Forces me into its image.

Urban Forest

growing strong without notice
weathering each season
sheltering strangers shading streets
anchored deep reaching high
standing still always moving

Aunty Elaine Lomas: Your Smile Is a River

Aunty Elaine,
Wiradjuri Yinaa of the Kalari/
freshwater woman/ from the heart of Country/ descended
from Goorawin & John Grant of Ireland/ Granddaughter
of William Patrick Grant – Lore & Law man storyteller
and drover/ Mother taken at eleven while her Father
was droving/ sent to Cootamundra Girls Home/ then to
service at thirteen at Angledool Station up north/ granted
permission to come home/

Aunty Elaine,
Wiradjuri Yinaa of the Kalari/
born on Country/ came home to a tent at Yenda/ orphaned at
two after her Mother's passing/ taken into the family of Uncle
Cecil/ strong in culture and Christianity/ sister to Uncles Cecil
Junior, Stan, Herb, Marvin and Ashley/ to Aunties Florence,
Lorna, Marie Ellen and Fay/ lived on Three Ways Reserve
Griffith/ spent her childhood rabbit-trapping/ with sister Flo
poked a goanna out of rabbit burrow for dinner/ heard the
Elders telling stories 'round the campfire/ thought she saw the
Mirrioola Dog in a paddock/

Aunty Elaine,
Wiradjuri Yinaa of the Kalari/
member of the Aborigines Inland Mission/ remembers when
Grandfather was sent to jail for speaking language while
just a few benches away languages from the Mediterranean
were freely spoken/ left school at fifteen/ combines Country
and Christian upbringing seamlessly/ went to Bible College

on Wonnarua Country/ travelled across the nation to be a missionary on Wongatha lands/ ate bush tucker for her twenty-first birthday/

Aunty Elaine,
Wiradjuri Yinaa of the Kalari/
became a nursing aide in Leonora over west/ left when asked to move a body before its spirit had left/ came back over east/ worked delivering babies in maternity/ was a NSW Aboriginal health trailblazer/ in 1977 became the first Aboriginal hospital liaison officer/ moved to Kambera on Ngunnawal Country/ worked for the National Aboriginal Community Controlled Health/

Aunty Elaine,
Wiradjuri Yinaa of the Kalari/
Mother of Catherine & George and Bethany & Dean/ Grandmother of Charlotte, Sienna, Bentley/ remembers Aunty Emmy and Aunty Sabina back in Condobolin speaking old words/ says learning language is like pouring honey from a jar into a glass bowl/ watching every drop ooze from jar to bowl/ knows when the bowl is full – she *is* that bowl/ when you know your language/ you are complete/ brings language to our youth in honour of Grandpa Johnson/ wants the young ones to know the past to understand the present to make the future/

Aunty Elaine,
Wiradjuri Yinaa of the Kalari/
knows that yesterday never ends and tomorrow is a precarious hope/ drives to Gundagai when she is homesick to dip her feet in the Murrumbidya/ wants her children and

children's children to have their lives free from surveillance/ speaks to herself in language when she is down/ Badhu Wiradjuri/ Badhu Dyiramadilinya/

Aunty Elaine,
Wiradjuri Yinaa of the Kalari/
Mother/ Grandmother/ Sister/ Aunty/ Elder/ Teacher/ Language Custodian/ who changes the world through small acts of kindness/ who brings two cultures together in spirituality/ whose smile is a river ancient and deep/ whose words will flow through generations to come like Kalari and Murrumbidya/

Sung by Birds

… searching for a poem
I sit on the edge of Country at daybreak
where river meets sea – fresh water and salt
birdsong stuns the winter air
magpies on electric wires staved out like time across
rose-grey canvas
ruby-billed black swans on the river inlet arch their long
slender necks like question marks asking all that is
unanswered of Australia
sooty oystercatchers on the shoreline sit like the black dots
of ellipses
the rest of the story unfinished
floats out on the open sea …

Of Colonial Poets and Bridges on Wiradjuri Country

The bridges were already built
the ballads already written for Gundagai –
colonial town above
a mighty river that forced it up a stony hill
a century before I was born

my grandmother never went to the convent school
on the hill where bricked-in by slate stone
like the jail next door
Irish nuns who'd never seen a snake
or a Blackfella before
taught us the history of nation

my grandmother said out here
is not god's country
the river sings a better hymn than any choir
these clouds are not hung
nor rocks or hills placed
for the colonial poet's eye

the river is the highest power
the bridge never held the water underneath it
the air does not hold these syllables
nor does Country remember their words.

Entanglement

the melding shade of river gum
and boughs of weeping willow gnarl
entangled roots deep through creek banks
entwined and curved in an earthy bed
they might almost be lovers in embrace

my bloodlines run deep through this creek
deep under granite veins that climb the hills
as they run across jagged wire fence lines
strung out like dirty tufts of wool on tetanus-barbs
invaded and invader knotted in unbreakable grip

to untangle this story of enmeshment between water,
land and wire to cut through this welded weave
of roots, invasion, blood on the ground
will bleed both gum and willow dry
and crumble the bank that holds their story

Yulany Dhabal

Yulany dhabal – skin and bone
dhaagun and *bunhaan* fly in the wind
dust and ash gather.
In the beginning *Baiame* turns
dust to skin makes living bone
to walk Country – to gather
scatter ashes to nourish.

Country is red dust gathered –
formed to rocks, sculpted to mountains,
hollowed to gullies – dug to rivers –
breathes life shapes its people to walk
leaving only dust – ashes to scatter
in the wind – to take only memories
gather up stories – track through
Country – tread lightly – carefully
across its Dreamings.

Your Last River

When a body is sick it lies in a bed.
Shrinks away. Is gone forever. The bed is empty.

When a river gets sick it loses colour. Fades.
Shrinks in its bed. Dries up. Dies.

Water has a perfect memory. The river says:
Remember me this way. Like I am your last river.

Gone is not forgotten but you can't drink
memory, nor will mourning quench your thirst.

Think of me. Like I am your future. Your
first and only love.

Like I am your last truth –
because I am.

Like you will die without me –
because you will.

Like I am your last river –
because I might be.

Still Gatherers

Inspired by 'Who's Afraid of Colour?' – Aboriginal Women's Art Exhibition National Gallery of Victoria 2017

Country's awash with the gatherings of Blak Women –
first gift to her children – rich offerings of place.
Yawk-Yawk spreads ancient wings –

breathes female spirits – sings:

Come – gather – bring together – create – give back –

forage your memories – take back this manhandled history

remember your dismembered Countries – rejuvenate this nation's space –

colour the whitewash – sing Country afresh.

We are here on rock, in sand, in soil, in grasses and reeds,
on wood, with clay, with paint, with print,

on canvas and silk, with string, in glass, on screen, through lens –

Gan'yu women interconnected – numerous as the stars in languages
of our land we say:

We are still gatherers – still custodians.

This is the strength of us – Blak Women!

We are strong –

bust up colonial myths – smash through glass ceilings –

disperse the gossip they call history.

Pick up the pieces of our Dreamings –

gather and create – erase that story that paints us wrong –

in layered textures tell our truths –

colours bold speak louder than words.

We speak through brush, through paint, through twine –
each pandanus fibre a story – each story a string –
each string a basket –

each basket holds what cannot be stolen –

our blood memories that pulse like the dancing lines

we paint, that hold us like the intricate baskets we weave,

that shape us like the clay we mould, the glass we meld.

Gather the refuse of colonialism,

the litter, the waste, rubbish and lies –

remould them, reshape them, refine them,

remake them –

pin the untruths of two centuries to the walls.

Gather and re-gather what was scattered for centuries
cast driftnets wide and deep bring back what was lost.
Make story – put back together the pieces –

nurture and heal like Blak Women can.

Gather memories, stories of Grandmothers,

Mothers, Aunties, Sisters, Daughters –

constellations of Blak Women shine out,

bring together – rewrite national narratives,

chronicle our genesis – project our future – gather old and new.

In creative solidarity we gather to tell –

keep telling, create – recreate.

We still are weavers, makers, keepers, tellers –

always will be givers, carers, dreamers, creators –

Blak Women – gatherers for all times.

… gather words
        upon pages
        untangle thoughts
make them speak …

Acknowledgements

This collection is a moment that is part of a much bigger momentum. It's gathering made possible and brought to fruition by the support and encouragement of many.

Much of this collection was written on the unceded lands of the East Kulin Nation of the Wurundjeri Peoples. I acknowledge the Wurundjeri Peoples for their continued care of Country, and for the privilege of living and working as a visitor on these lands. I'd also like to acknowledge that some of these works were written on Wiradjuri Country – my home Country between Wagga Wagga and Gundagai; and that some works were written while on residencies on Dharug and Gundungurra Country, Ngunnawal and Ngambri Country, and Dharawal and Dhurga Country.

I am grateful to have received support from several writers' residencies and fellowships over the last few years that allowed me the space and time to work on new poems that came together to make this collection. I'd like to acknowledge Red Room Poetry for always encouraging my poetry and for their generous fellowship, which I received in 2019 for my project *Voicing the Unsettled Space: Rewriting the Colonial Mythscape*; and the two-week residency and fellowship at Bundanon Trust where I wrote several poems that appear in 'Nation'; to Varuna Writers' House for two residencies – one in 2020, which was much needed after the confinement of Covid lockdowns, and another in 2022, where I wrote several new poems for *Gawimarra* – and who also awarded me an international residency at Cove Park, Scotland, where I completed the final edits for this collection; and to Booranga Writers' Centre, Wagga Wagga, where I spent two weeks on Country in the winter of 2021, and where I got to experience the majesty of the Murrumbidgee in flood again after many years, and roamed around the hills, valleys and plains of Wiradjuri Country to feel its power from sole to soul.

Special acknowledgement and gratitude to Wiradjuri Elder and language custodian Aunty Elaine Lomas, who gave me some language – beautiful Wiradjuri words, which should have been my birthright but weren't due to the invasion and colonial history of this nation. Thanks to Gunai poet and author Kirli Saunders, who invited me to participate in Red Room's Poetry in First Languages initiative in 2018; and to the late great Aunty Kerry Reed-Gilbert, who introduced me to Aunty Elaine. Red Room Poetry generously provided financial support and encouragement for the interpretations offered by Aunty Elaine. Working with Aunty Elaine and learning even just a few Wiradjuri words has been a life-changing experience for me. And this experience has steeled my determination to learn and to speak the Wiradjuri language that should have been my first language.

I'd like to thank Bundjalung poet, scholar and friend Evelyn Araluen, who in 2021 encouraged me to pull all the poems that I had written since my last collection, *Walk Back Over* (Cordite Books, 2018), into a new collection and enter the 2021 Helen Anne Bell Poetry Prize for an unpublished manuscript; and for assisting me in curating all the poems I had written since 2018 – which, as Evelyn predicted, was more than I thought. The manuscript was shortlisted for the Helen Anne Bell Prize; was awarded the Sydney University School of Literature, Art and Media Poetry Award and was then accepted by University of Queensland Press for publication. Without Evelyn's encouragement this collection probably wouldn't have happened.

Thanks to Mununjali poet, writer and friend Ellen van Neerven, who provided careful, thoughtful editorial advice and much-needed, valued suggestions on this collection, which is sharper as a result of Ellen's care and attention to detail. They also encouraged me to write several new pieces, which made *Gawimarra* a stronger, more substantial collection in the end.

Thank you to Aviva Tuffield from UQP, who read the original manuscript, and who offered me further encouragement and a publishing contract. Thanks to editor Yasmin Smith from UQP for her work on the later drafts of this collection. Yasmin's laser-eye and experience as an editor of First Nations writing greatly benefitted this manuscript in its final stages. Thanks to Ian See, who proofread the final version of *Gawimarra*. Much gratitude and appreciation to graphic artist Lily Sawenko, who designed the cover, and who gave me many thoughtful and beautiful concepts to think about before I eventually settled on the stunning cover that you see.

Several poems in this collection have appeared as standalone works in literary journals and/or online poetry sites such as *Overland Literary Journal*, *Hecate*, *Best of Australian Poems 2021*, *Rabbit*, *Cordite Poetry Review* and Red Room Poetry.

Other works were commissioned for specific projects in art galleries and museums, such as Murray Art Museum Albury, Bathurst Regional Art Gallery and the National Gallery of Victoria. I acknowledge and thank all these publications and platforms for encouraging, promoting and supporting my work.

Last, but by no means least, I want to thank from the bottom of my heart my family, who have always believed in me as a writer – even when I didn't – and who are the reason I keep going and growing not just in writing but in life. I acknowledge my children, Jerome, Eugene and Hugo, for their support and inspiration, and my husband of many decades, Peter, who is always so solid like the rock from which he takes his name.

Mandaang guwu to everyone who has made this gathering possible.